First World War
and Army of Occupation
War Diary
France, Belgium and Germany

58 DIVISION
Divisional Troops
504 Field Company Royal Engineers
1 September 1915 - 29 February 1916

WO95/2996/3

The Naval & Military Press Ltd
www.nmarchive.com
Published in association with The National Archives

Published by

The Naval & Military Press Ltd

Unit 10 Ridgewood Industrial Park,

Uckfield, East Sussex,

TN22 5QE England

Tel: +44 (0) 1825 749494

www.naval-military-press.com

www.nmarchive.com

This diary has been reprinted in facsimile from the original. Any imperfections are inevitably reproduced and the quality may fall short of modern type and cartographic standards.

© Crown Copyright
Images reproduced by permission of The National Archives, London, England, 2015.

Contents

Document type	Place/Title	Date From	Date To
Heading	WO95/2996/3		
Heading	58th Division 504th Field Coy. R.E. 1915 Sep-1916 Feb And 1917 Jan-1919 May		
Miscellaneous	Monthly Statement	02/09/1915	02/09/1915
War Diary	Wickham Market	01/09/1915	01/10/1915
War Diary	Needham Market	02/10/1915	29/02/1916

WO 95/2996/3

58TH DIVISION

504TH FIELD COY. R.E.
~~JAN 1917 - MAY 1919.~~

1915 SEP — 1916 FEB
and
1917 JAN — 1919 MAY

Monthly Statement

Unit. 2/2nd London Field Coy R.E.
Div: 58" (London)
Mobilization Centre. 10. Victoria Park Square London E
Temporary War Station. Wickham Market.
Stations occupied since Mobilization. Maidstone, Lenham, Buxted, Macesfield Crowborough Norwich, Brightlingsea, Ipswich

g. Reorganization of T.F. into Home & Imperial Service

Home Service men to the number of 42% of the establishment of the company which is complete are still administered by the Company staff although under another command. This entails very considerable additional time & labour.

It is recommended that Home Service R.E. be transferred as pioneers to Provisional Battalions or formed into composite Fortress Companies for Coast Defence.

Wickham Market
2/9/15

G. T. Kingsfield
MAJOR R.E., T.,
O.C., 2nd/2nd LONDON FIELD CO.

WAR DIARY
or
INTELLIGENCE SUMMARY

Army Form C. 2118.

2/2nd London Field Coy RE

Place	Date	Hour	Summary of Events and Information	Remarks and references to Appendices
Wickham Market	1/9/15		Technical training in defence Woodbridge-Saxmundary. 2/Lt PA Seurat reported for duty.	SD6
	2/9		Technical training in defence Woodbridge - Saxmundary. Patrolling. Inters[?]	SD6
	3/9		Adjuraning 2/Lt Byron McCallum to proceed as reinforcement to 1/2nd London Fd Coy. Orders received for detachment to proceed to Grapham for Musketry. Musketry instruction.	SD6
	4/9		Instruction, review Musketry training.	SD6
	5/9		Church Parade. Orders received postponing entrainment of Lt. Byron McCallum to 8th inst.	SD6
	6/9		Detachment for Musketry left for Grapham under 2/Lt Velia & Seurat. 2/Lt Harton reported for duty.	SD6
	7/9		Mounted men returns from Grapham on completion of course. Departure 2/Lt Byron McCallum to transport.	SD6
	8/9		2nd party mounted men under 2/Lieut Bonne proceeds Grapham to Musketry. Warning of Zeppelin raid received 9.45 pm. Action taken under recent order.	SD6

Army Form C. 2118.

WAR DIARY
or
INTELLIGENCE SUMMARY.
(Erase heading not required.)

Instructions regarding War Diaries and Intelligence Summaries are contained in F.S. Regs., Part II. and the Staff Manual respectively. Title pages will be prepared in manuscript.

Place	Date	Hour	Summary of Events and Information	Remarks and references to Appendices
Wulham Market	9/9/15		Relief of 2nd pack mounts been on completion of Musketry at Lyndham. Warning 1 Zeppelin raid 9.15 pm. Action taken as before.	7D2
	10/9		Detachment returned from Musketry at Lyndham. Reorganisation in Musketry Instruction in Companies until — Kit room inspection. Leave to Bury.	7D2
	11/9		Church Parade	7D2
	12/9			7D2
	13/9		Technical Training Rafting, defence of landing, little bridging. Warning received 8.20. Action taken as before.	7D2 7D2
	14/9		Technical Training as on 13/9/15	7D2
	15/9		" " " Warning of raid received 8.15 pm Action taken as before	5D4
	16/9		Technical Training as on 13/9/15	5D6
	17/9		Company Drill — Kit room inspection — Manner Musketry. Review. Issues of Pay.	7D2
	18/9		Section Route Marches. Orders received 6 pm to prepare for Technical Exercise. C Co packs & ready to move at 8.30 pm.	5D2

A.D.S.S./Forms/C. 2118.

Army Form C. 2118.

WAR DIARY
or
INTELLIGENCE SUMMARY.
(Erase heading not required.)

Place	Date	Hour	Summary of Events and Information	Remarks and references to Appendices
Welldam Market	19/9/15		Church Parade. Coy Staring by.	TDC
	20/9		Coy Staring by. Musketry & Manual instruction. 2.30 pm helpers	TDC
	21/9		perm Vigilance run. Unexpected.	TDC
	22/9		Technical Training defence of building - Spar hedging	TDC
	23/9		"	TDC
	24/9		Coy drin - Manoeuvres, Kit Inspection - Pay parade	TDC
	25/9		Sector Road Marches	TDC
	26/9		Church parade.	TDC
	27/9		Preparation for move - Clearing field works & washing ports	TDC
	28/9		"	TDC
	29/9		"	TDC
	30/9		"	TDC

G.T. Muggspud
MAJOR R.E., T.,
O.C., 2nd/2nd LONDON FIELD CO.

Confidential

Army Form C. 2118.

2/2nd London Field Coy

WAR DIARY
INTELLIGENCE SUMMARY.
(Erase heading not required.)

Instructions regarding War Diaries and Intelligence Summaries are contained in F. S. Regs., Part II. and the Staff Manual respectively. Title pages will be prepared in manuscript.

Place	Date	Hour	Summary of Events and Information	Remarks and references to Appendices
WICKHAM MARKET	1/10/15	6 p.m.	Orders received to prepare reinforcement of 27 Dismounted + 20 Mounted Men for 1/2nd London Field Coy RE.	TDC
NEEDHAM MARKET	2/10/15		More of Company with Hd RE & 2/1st London Field Coy RE & NEEDHAM MARKET	TDC
	3-4/10/15		Nil	TDC
	5/10/15		2/Lt P.A. Fount RE relinquishes Commission	TDC
	6/10/15		Nil	TDC
	7/10/15		Capt. A.O. Laird RE reported for duty	TDC
	8-10/10/15		Nil	TDC
	11/10/15		Orders received to mounted officer as reinforcement. Lt G.B. Harden RE reinforcement	TDC
	12-17/10/15		Nil	TDC
	18/10/15		Orders received for departure of draft 1/ Officer & 47 other ranks	TDC
	19/10/15	7.23 p.m.	Draft 1 + 47 other ranks under command Lt G.B. Harden left for port of Embarkation	TDC
	20-23/10		Nil	TDC
	24/10	4 p.m.	Orders received for Major G.T. Kingspie RE nominated Major G.T. Kingspie RE nominated as reinforcement	TDC
	25-26/10		Nil	TDC
	27/10		Notification Major G.T. Kingspie not required. Orders revised.	TDC
	28-31/10		Nil	TDC

G.T. Kingspie
Major R.E.

Army Form C. 2118.

WAR DIARY
or
INTELLIGENCE SUMMARY.
2/2nd London Field
(Erase heading not required.)

Place	Date	Hour	Summary of Events and Information	Remarks and references to Appendices
NEEDHAM MARKET	1/11/15		Nil.	
	2/11/15		2/Lt C.A.T. Sain reported for duty.	TDC
	5/11/15			TDC
	6/11/15 to 30/11/15		Nil	TDC

Needham Market
1/12/15

G.T.Ringshaw
MAJOR R.E., i.,
O.C., 2nd/2nd LONDON FIELD CO

Army Form C. 2118.

WAR DIARY
or
INTELLIGENCE SUMMARY. 2/2nd London Fd Coy R.E.

(Erase heading not required.)

Instructions regarding War Diaries and Intelligence Summaries are contained in F. S. Regs., Part II. and the Staff Manual respectively. Title pages will be prepared in manuscript.

Place	Date	Hour	Summary of Events and Information	Remarks and references to Appendices
NEEDHAM MARKET	1/1/16 to 13/1/16		N.I.	
	14/1/16		2/Lt. Penrock reported for duty	
	15/1/16 to 31/1/16		N.I.	

G.T. Phugofer
MAJOR R.E.,
O.C., 2nd/2nd LONDON FIELD CO.
3/1/16

[Stamp: 58th (LONDON) DIVISION — 4 JAN 1916 — GEN. STAFF]

Secret

Army Form C. 2118.

WAR DIARY

INTELLIGENCE SUMMARY

2/2nd London Field Coy R.E.

(Erase heading not required.)

Place	Date	Hour	Summary of Events and Information	Remarks and references to Appendices
NEEDHAM MARKET	1/1/16 to 14/1/16		Nil	T.K.
	15/1/16		Orders received to limit to prepare for service overseas	T.K.
	16/1/16 to 31/1/16		Nil	T.K.

[Stamp: 66th (2nd East Anglian) Division 3 FEB 1916 GENERAL STAFF]

G.T. Pingstone
MAJOR R.E.,
O.C., 2nd/2nd LONDON FIELD CO

2/2/16

Army Form C. 2118.

WAR DIARY
or
INTELLIGENCE SUMMARY. 2/2 Wessex Field. Co. RE

(Erase heading not required.)

Instructions regarding War Diaries and Intelligence Summaries are contained in F. S. Regs., Part II and the Staff Manual respectively. Title pages will be prepared in manuscript.

Hour, Date, Place	Summary of Events and Information	Remarks and references to Appendices
NEEDHAM MARKET		
23.2.16 2.30 AM	Unit arrived from SOUTHBOURNE.	
24.2.16 to 29.2.16	Nil	

J R War Armstrong Capt
O.C. 2ND Wx. Fd. Coy. R.E.

NEEDHAM MARKET
2.3.16.